D.E.T.A.C.H.
Deny Earthly Things As Christ Has

How to Develop a Biblical Mindset for Personal Finance

JONATHAN SAYLES

Copyright © 2015 by Jonathan Sayles

D.E.T.A.C.H. Deny Earthly Things As Christ Has
How to Develop a Biblical Mindset for Personal Finance

by Jonathan Sayles

Printed in the United States of America.

ISBN 9781498442862

All rights reserved solely by the author. The author guarantees all contents are original and do not infringe upon the legal rights of any other person or work. No part of this book may be reproduced in any form without the permission of the author. The views expressed in this book are not necessarily those of the publisher.

Unless otherwise indicated, all Scripture quotations are taken from the King James Version *(KJV) – public domain*.

Scripture quotations marked NIV are taken from The Holy Bible, New International Version®, NIV® Copyright © 1973, 1978, 1984, 2011 by Biblica, Inc.® Used by permission. All rights reserved worldwide.

www.xulonpress.com

To

Jessica, my wife and Joanna, my daughter

TABLE OF CONTENTS

Acknowledgements ix
Introduction: Why I Decided to Write
        This Book xiii

Chapter 1: Blindsided 15
Chapter 2: D.E.T.A.C.H. 29
Chapter 3: Examining Yourself 43
Chapter 4: Setting Priorities 53
Chapter 5: Determining to Free Yourself 61
Chapter 6: Practicing Contentment 81
Chapter 7: Living for God's Kingdom 89

About the Author 107
Appendix 109
Endnotes 115

ACKNOWLEDGEMENTS

There have been so many people who have helped me throughout my life. Many of them have helped me greatly in ministry as well. Let me start by thanking my Lord and Savior Jesus Christ first. Jesus Christ has transformed my life from the inside out. I will forever be grateful for what Jesus did for me on the cross.

Next, I would like to thank my wife, Jessica. You have loved me, supported me and served me with more grace than I deserve. You are such a godly woman and an awesome mother. It is such a joy to be your husband. I love you so much!

Then, I would like to thank my daughter, Joanna. You are my first child, and currently my only child. Even though you are currently only one year old, you speak to me with such cheerfulness. I will always do the best that I can to raise you up to follow Jesus Christ. I love you!

Mom and Dad, thank you for standing with me throughout my life and putting up with me during my teenage years. Mom, thank you for your constant love. And Dad, even though you have gone to be with Jesus in Heaven, thank you for instilling hard work, discipline and Christianity into me. I am forever grateful for being raised in a godly home by such wonderful, God-fearing parents.

The rest of my family, my brothers Will and Everett, and my sister Connie, thank you for always looking out for me. To all of my extended family, I am grateful to be a part of such a loving family.

I want to thank my spiritual mentors who helped me as I was starting out in ministry. My dad's pastor, Pastor Joe Howard, Pastor Dennis Watson and Pastor Manley Miller. Thank you for your encouragement and biblical wisdom and insight.

Thanks to the many others who helped me out when starting in ministry including Barry

Acknowledgements

Haindel, Archie Corder, Pastor Michael Sprague, Michelle Geoffrey, Pastor Tony Leverett, my church family at Celebration Church, Christian Evangelical Ministries, Pastor Roland Williams, Mary Williams, all of the board members of our ministry, and all of our financial partners in ministry who give generously to support the work that we are doing for God's kingdom.

I want to thank everyone else who has helped me. I am not intending on leaving anyone out. You know exactly who you are. Finally, thanks to everyone who, after reading this book, will D.E.T.A.C.H. for the sake of the kingdom of God!

INTRODUCTION:
Why I Decided to Write This Book

One random day, I was driving down a boulevard near my home and I began to think about helping people. I had been in the financial planning industry for six years and I just was discouraged by so many of the stories I was coming across. I met with many families and individuals to help them set goals and plan their personal finances. What discouraged me was that many people were in similar situations. They had not been educated on personal finance, and many had fallen into the trap of doing what everyone else around them seemed to be doing with their finances. The problem was that everyone else around them was broke.

Suddenly, the Lord brought to my mind the word detach. This was interesting because when I really began to think about it, this was the reason that so many people were struggling with their money and possessions. A few moments later, I began to think about a way to make it memorable. Soon thereafter, I came up with D.eny E.arthly T.hings A.s C.hrist H.as. This began to make a lot of sense to me because, in most cases, this is what that individual or family needed to hear to help them understand how to develop a biblical mindset for their personal finances. Many of the common questions that people needed answered were as follows: Why am I not happy or content? Why is it hard for me to give? Why can't I have what my neighbors have? Why is it so hard for me to save money? Do I have too much money? What can I do to handle my finances in a way that honors God? These are some of the questions that I believe you will be able to answer for yourself after reading this book. My prayer is that Christians, churches, and organizations all over the world will D.E.T.A.C.H., and we will see the kingdom of God expand like never before!

Chapter 1:

Blindsided

In the summer of 2012, I attended a mission trip to Mexico. I actually did not want to go or plan to go. I was working in the investment business and I was planning to speak at a state convention for one of my target markets. This was their annual convention and they asked me if I could speak about financial planning. "Are you kidding?" I said, "Absolutely! I will do it!" It was a HUGE opportunity! That event was definitely all over my calendar and I was not going to remove it for anything. Or so I thought.

One Wednesday at noontime, I went to a Christian Business Men's lunch and a friend of mine named Archie asked me if I was going to be able to go on the mission trip to Mexico. It was going to be a vacation Bible school. This was probably his seventh or eighth time asking me and, quite frankly, I wanted him to stop asking me. I said that I couldn't because I was building a business and I had this HUGE opportunity to speak at a statewide annual conference to promote my investment business. He replied by stating that he understood because he was an entrepreneur himself.

When I got back to my office, I had an email from the conference committee stating that they did not need me to speak any more. Boy, was I upset! I couldn't believe that they would take me out of the program because their "main" speaker wanted more time. A flurry of emotions and thoughts went through my mind. "Why me? This is not fair. What did I do wrong?"

A few hours later, I began to wonder if God was trying to tell me to go on this mission trip. "No way," I thought. I had just spoken to Archie earlier that morning and I told him that I could not go. However, eventually, I realized that God did want me to go on this mission trip to Reynosa, Mexico with Archie and the mission team from his church. Thus, I reluctantly called Archie and signed up for the trip.

There were two meetings at the church for the mission team to prepare and organize what we needed for the trip. Everyone was assigned to different tasks for the different stations that we were going to set up at the different churches in Mexico. At first, I was kind of upset because I wouldn't be able to access my phone. There was no way that I was going to pay the rate for international cell phone minutes with my carrier. Next, I found out that I couldn't drink the water. I was even going to need to use bottled water to brush my teeth! This was frustrating. However, I should have known this about Mexico, but I did not realize it until I actually started planning to go to Mexico. This was my first time ever going to Mexico. In fact, it was my first time ever leaving the United States. Later, I found out that I would not be able to put toilet paper in the toilet. I just thought, "What in the world did I sign up for?" Nevertheless, I was going to obey God, and go on this trip.

On departure day, we met at the church first and then we carpooled together to the airport for our early morning flight. Our first flight was on a large airplane from New Orleans, LA to Houston, TX. We then had less than an hour to scamper across the George Bush Intercontinental Airport to catch our connecting fight to McAllen, TX. After we landed in McAllen, we were picked up by one of the missionary families that we would be serving with. We had to load all of the luggage and about 15 people into two SUVs. One was a Ford Expedition and another was a 12 passenger van. We did this while it was extremely hot in McAllen, TX. Next, we headed to a church in McAllen to pick up some supplies for one of the other missionaries that was hosting our team. Once again we were loading supplies in the heat. Then, we still had plenty of supplies to get, so we headed to Walmart to get all of the food and supplies needed for the vacation Bible school. At Walmart, we were also able to get something to eat at the McDonald's inside of the Walmart. From there, we drove across the border to Reynosa, Mexico to the bunkhouse that we were going to stay in for the next four days.

When we arrived in Reynosa, many of the mission team members and I were very tired. I assumed that our work was done for the day and all that was left to do was eat and go to sleep. However, there was more to the rest of the day. We went to the kitchen for dinner. To my surprise, dinner was very delicious. Next, we went to the home church of one of the missionary families where the father was the pastor. The worship service was amazing! They must have prepared for us because they would sing part of the song in Spanish and then sing the same verse in English. This was a very nice surprise. We stayed to hear a short message, and afterwards, we were able to fellowship with their church members. They were very joyful and greeted us cordially. Next, we drove back to the bunkhouse. I was preparing to shower and go to sleep, however, we were not done yet. We had one more task. We had to prepare all of our materials for the next day. All of the arts, crafts, games, clothes and giveaways had to be ready to go for the next morning. This was tiring as well. After setting up, I went to take a shower. It wasn't the cleanest place, so I was a little squeamish. I am a bit of a germophobe, so I was starting to feel like I was going to die from too many germs. Nevertheless,

I made it through the shower and went to sleep at about midnight. Most of the other members of the mission team went to bed between 11:00 pm and midnight as well.

The next morning I awoke just in time. I quickly got ready and ate breakfast, had Bible reading and devotional, and loaded our supplies for our vacation Bible school at the first church that we were going to serve at. Typically, I don't eat breakfast, but I ate that day because I wanted to see what a traditional Mexican breakfast would taste like. To my surprise, again, it was very enjoyable. So far, I was happy about one thing on this mission trip: good food. When the missionaries arrived, we loaded all of the supplies into the vehicles and headed off to our first destination. After driving for a few minutes, we began to enter into a poverty stricken neighborhood. The roads were so rough that I do not believe they were EVER paved. I'm from New Orleans and we have some of the worst potholes in the street that I have ever seen. Yet, they are nowhere near as bad as the streets in Mexico. I began to see some terrible looking structures that ended up being their housing. Some were made up of old wood, some aluminum, and some were made from cinder blocks. My heart was broken. We arrived at the church to see kids playing in the field of rocks right next to it. The church was made of aluminum and the roof did not cover the entire church. My heart was flooded with compassion for the people in that neighborhood. There is NO PLACE in the United States that has poverty even close to what I saw that day. After the initial shock, I began to settle down. We set up the first part of the vacation Bible school, which was a Bible story taught by Mr. Dave, one of our mission team members. He did an awesome job! My assignment was to help with the games and then the arts and crafts. As I began to serve and minister to the children in this impoverished community, my heart was filled with joy. I began to have basic conversations with them in Spanish. The Spanish that I had learned in high school and college started coming back to me a little at a time. The missionaries helped me translate when it was something that I couldn't remember how to say. Many of the children wanted to take pictures with me, so I did. They also taught me the "man's Mexican handshake." It was UNBELIEVEABLE how happy and joyful I felt.

After this vacation Bible school session, we went back to the bunkhouse for lunch and to prepare for the next church we would serve at. Lunch was a basic sandwich and chips. This was the first meal that was not Mexican. We took a short break, and then it was time to prepare again for the afternoon church that we were going to serve. We loaded up the van and we were off to our 2nd vacation Bible school location. Once again, we rode on terrible streets and saw terrible living conditions. After we arrived and set up, Mr. Dave began to tell the Bible story. After the story, the children split up into different groups for the different areas including arts, crafts, games, face painting and coloring. I was at the crafts table this time, and I began to feel overwhelmed with joy as I was able to serve these children and reflect the joy of the Lord to them. My Spanish speaking had improved a little bit more, so I connected more with the children by speaking their language. We ended with giving the children items to put in their bags including toothpaste, toothbrushes, socks, pencils, stuffed animals, combs and snacks. As we finished, I thought about what I heard a World War II veteran say, "We had a job to do and we did it!" I shouted that to my friend Archie as we were leaving and he liked the saying. I let him know where I got it from and he began to use that saying as well. It became our saying at the end of every vacation Bible school that we completed. Next, we packed up and got into our vehicles to head back to the bunkhouse.

As we arrived, there was a pleasant aroma coming from the kitchen. It was more Mexican food! I didn't know what it was, but I know it had to be better than the ham and cheese sandwich with chips that we had for lunch. This time it was tamales. These tamales were the best that I had ever tasted. There was also a homemade salsa on the side. It was the best fresh salsa that I had ever eaten. After dinner, we had our typical evening devotional time. As I was getting tired and sleepy, I just realized that there was one more thing to do. We had to prepare all of the materials for the next day. After preparing the materials, it was time to take my shower. I cringed a little when thinking about the amount of germs in the bathroom, however, I made it through the shower once again. This time I was able to get to bed at about 10:30 pm, which was much better.

The next morning went the same as the day before. I almost forgot to use bottled water when brushing my teeth, but one of the mission team members reminded me just in time. Boy, was that scary! We went to a church in the morning and I was overtaken by the joy of the Lord while ministering to these children. We came back for sandwiches and chips for lunch. We prepared for the afternoon location and drove down horrible streets to get there. However, this location was not a church it was an orphanage. This was a different type of orphanage because some children technically did have parents. However, their parents were in tough situations. Some could not afford to feed and take care of their children. Others had a mother who was a prostitute and/or addicted to drugs. My heart was broken again. Nevertheless, as these children came up to me and starting playing with me and hugging me, I was inundated with joy, peace and happiness. When I thought about these kids, I was reminded of James 1:27, *Pure religion and undefiled before*

God and the Father is this, to visit the fatherless and widows in their affliction, and to keep himself unspotted from the world.

After we left the orphanage, we returned to the bunkhouse and ate a delicious home cooked Mexican meal. We had our evening devotional and prepared for the next day. Once again, by God's grace, I made it through the shower and went to sleep at about 10:00 pm.

The next morning, I woke up at about 5:00 am. I was able to have my quiet time and read my Bible by myself. I felt refreshed by God's word. This trip was getting more exciting. After reading my Bible and having my prayer time with the Lord, I brushed my teeth (with bottled water), washed my face, and changed into my clothes for the day. We ate another amazing breakfast, loaded up, and went to the last location for our vacation Bible school. This location was not a church. It was a community playground with a small building that was run by the government. The total building was probably about 600 square feet. We had to squeeze the kids inside for Mr. Dave's Bible story and afterwards, set up cramped stations for arts, crafts, games and coloring. The kids were so happy to see us. It was no surprise that I was filled with God's peace and joy. We finished by giving out all the rest of the toothpaste, toothbrushes, socks, pencils, stuffed animals, combs and snacks. Some of the parents wanted the hygiene items as well, so they received some of the items too. What an amazing finish to an awesome vacation Bible school!

We returned for our normal "American" lunch consisting of a sandwich and chips. For the afternoon, we were going to go to the shops in Nuevo Progreso. I picked up a few souvenir gifts, with my favorite being a Mexican molcajete. This was a type of bowl used to make some of the homemade salsa. This was a touristy area, so there were many stores along with Mexicans on the sidewalks trying to sell many different items including candy, gum, pottery, clothes and other souvenir type gifts. After a few hours, we headed back to the bunkhouse.

When we arrived, I was familiar with the aroma coming from the kitchen. We were having tacos. The tacos were awesome and the homemade salsa was very fresh. One of the Mexican ladies cleaned my molcajete for me and made me a very spicy salsa. This salsa was very good, but extremely HOT! I relied on some of the other mission team members to help me eat it all. After dinner, one of the missionary families presented each of us with a gift from the members at their church. This was unbelievable! These people did not have much, but they were determined to give each one of us a gift to show their appreciation. I was touched. As I was getting sleepy, I realized that we did not have anything else to do before my shower. We did not have to prepare for any vacation Bible schools for the next day. We stayed up and shared our thoughts and experiences with each other after an evening devotional. It seemed that everyone was encouraged and blessed by this awesome experience!

On the last morning, I woke up early and read my Bible. I was refreshed again by the nourishment from God's word. I then packed and prepared for breakfast. We said our goodbyes and took pictures with the mission team and missionary families. I believe we were all equally sad that it was time to leave. Before we went to the airport, we stopped in on a Sunday service of one of the famous churches in the area. The worship blew my socks off! We were only able to stay for part of the message so that we could be on time for our flight. However, I really enjoyed the service.

On our flight home, I was reminiscing about my incredible experiences over the last few days. Suddenly, I was blindsided by God! I did not see this coming! God had just revealed something to me. I was actually okay with not being able to use my cell phone, only drinking bottled water, and not being able to put toilet paper in the toilet. Did something change? Did I miss something? What had happened to me? I had D.E.T.A.C.H.ed and Denied Earthly Things As Christ Has....

Chapter 2:

D.E.T.A.C.H.-Deny Earthly Things As Christ Has

Deny Earthly Things

The Merriam-Webster dictionary defines the word deny as follows: "to restrain (oneself) from gratification of desires." No one likes to restrain themselves including me. Its definition for detach is "to separate (yourself) *from* someone or something." What I am saying with D.E.T.A.C.H. is that we should restrain ourselves from our desires of attaching our worth and significance to earthly things. We should detach or separate ourselves from the mindset that our significance in life is measured by acquiring earthly things and earthly possessions. There is nothing wrong with having "stuff," but it becomes a problem when the "stuff" has you.

Jesus talked about denying yourself in the Bible. Matthew 16:24 reads, *Then said Jesus unto his disciples, If any man will come after me, let him deny himself, and take up his cross, and follow me.* You can't claim to be a true follower of Jesus if you cannot or will not deny yourself. Overcoming self and denying yourself are by no means easy. We need the help of the Lord Jesus and the power of the Holy Spirit.

In Luke chapter 5, Jesus calls his first disciples. I will paraphrase verses 1 through 10. Jesus was standing by the lake of Gennesaret where a crowd of people gathered around him wanting to hear the Word of God. Jesus saw two boats where the fishermen were outside of the boats and washing the nets. He entered Simon's boat and taught the people from the boat. After teaching, he told Simon to go out into the deep water and let down the nets. Simon responded to him stating that they had worked all night and did not catch anything, but he would obey him nevertheless. When he let down the nets, there

D.E.T.A.C.H.–Deny Earthly Things As Christ Has

were so many fish that the nets began to break. They called their partners to come and help them and they filled both of the ships until they began to sink. Simon Peter fell down at Jesus' feet and asked Jesus to leave him because he was a sinful man. Everyone with him was amazed. Jesus told them not to fear and from now on they would catch men. Verse 11 picks up, *And when they had brought their ships to land, they forsook all, and followed him.* To forsake all means to leave everything. They did not go back and get their best supplies or favorite items. They did not go back and make an announcement or get two weeks to prepare. At that very moment, they were immediately willing to D.E.T.A.C.H. and leave EVERYTHING!

The Rich Young Ruler

There is a great example in the Bible about denying yourself, and many people refer to this particular passage as the rich young ruler. In the gospel of Mark, it is recorded in Chapter 10. Verses 17-27 read, *[17] And when he was gone forth into the way, there came one running, and kneeled to him, and asked him, Good Master, what shall I do that I may inherit eternal life? [18] And Jesus said unto him, Why callest thou me good? there is none good but one, that is, God. [19] Thou knowest the commandments, Do not commit adultery, Do not kill, Do not steal, Do not bear false witness, Defraud not, Honour thy father and mother. [20] And he answered and said unto him, Master, all these have I observed from my youth. [21] Then Jesus beholding him loved him, and said unto him, One thing thou lackest: go thy way, sell whatsoever thou hast, and give to the poor, and thou shalt have treasure in heaven: and come, take up the cross, and follow me. [22] And he was sad at that saying, and went away grieved: for he had great possessions. [23] And Jesus looked round about, and saith unto his disciples, How hardly shall they that have riches enter into the kingdom of God! [24] And the disciples were astonished at his words. But Jesus answereth again, and saith unto them, Children, how hard is it for them that trust in riches to enter into the kingdom of God! [25] It is easier for a camel to go through the eye of a needle, than for a rich man to enter into the kingdom of God. [26] And they were astonished out of measure, saying among themselves, Who then can be saved? [27] And Jesus looking upon them saith, With men it is impossible, but not with God: for with God all things are possible.*

Let's discuss what is happening in this passage. The rich young man runs up to Jesus and asks Jesus what he needed to do to inherit eternal life. Jesus responds by telling him the commandments, which the young man already knows. The young man responds by saying that he has kept these commandments since his youth. How likely was this 100% true? Not very likely. However, Jesus doesn't even address the truth to that statement. Jesus loved him, but he knew the young rich man's heart. He tells him that he lacks one thing. Jesus tells him to *"Sell all of your possessions, give to the poor, take up the cross, and follow me."* Then, the young man walked away sad because he had many possessions. In that moment, the rich young ruler would not D.E.T.A.C.H. Jesus then makes the famous statement, *"How hardly shall they that have riches enter in the kingdom of God."* Later, in verse 25, is another popular statement of Jesus, *"It is easier for a camel to go through the eye of a needle, than for a rich man to enter into the kingdom of God."* The disciples then respond by asking who then could be saved. Jesus ends this passage by saying, *"With men it is impossible, but not with God: for with God all things are possible."* Jesus never said that it was impossible for a rich man to be saved. He only said that it is hard. Many people use this passage to say that a rich man cannot go to heaven. However, this is an incorrect statement. Verse 24 is an important verse that many people don't pay attention to. Jesus says, *"How hard is it for them that **trust** in riches to enter into the kingdom of God"* [emphasis mine]. The key word here is trust. There is nothing wrong with wealth or riches. The problem is when someone begins to trust wealth or riches rather than trusting in Jesus Christ. Their view is that their entire identity is determined by how wealthy they are. They believe that they do not need God as long as they have a large amount of money and possessions. This is what makes it hard for rich people. It is very hard to overcome the temptation and lure of riches. However, with God all things are possible.

Case Examples

My background was meeting with individuals and families as a financial advisor before I obeyed God's call into the full-time ministry of Kingdom Financial Education. I have met with hundreds of individuals and families regarding many financial subjects including budgeting, saving, debt, insurance and retirement planning. Many times a couple could not make ends meet and they were forced to make choices. One piece of advice I had to give very often was to encourage them to get out of debt. I would explain the benefits of getting out of debt and they would agree. The individual or couple would say something like this, "This sounds great! What steps do we need to take?" This is usually where the conversation turned. Many times I would advise them to sell their brand new car and get a used car. This was a hot button. They would say to me, but we "need" a newer and safer car. We don't "need" to have a car that may need repairs here and there.

This happened many times again and again with different individuals and couples. What happened? Now, as I think back to many of these conversations, I realize that they did not want to D.E.T.A.C.H. They would not separate themselves from that new car.

Another example was from a lady in one of my classes. Through the ministry of Kingdom Financial Education, we offer an 8 week course called Kingdom Financial College. I teach this course to teach people how to handle their finances God's way. We were on the debt lesson and I began to explain some choices that people might have to make to get out of debt and do it in a short period of time. She blurted out, "I'm not giving up cable! I just don't care. I'm not giving up my cable!" I was speaking to the group and not to her personally. She shouted this out in front of everybody. We all laughed about it, but everyone understood the point that I was making. She was telling the group and herself that she was not willing to detach from cable television.

One more example is from my early days of being in the life insurance business. Many times, I would meet with a husband and a wife at their kitchen table. When getting a quote for them both, one of the key questions asks if they are a smoker or not. This is a huge deal because term life insurance rates for smokers are usually more than 100% more than the rates for non-smokers. For example, a non-smoker rate may be $50 per month and a smoker rate is typically more than $100 per month for the same coverage. Based on the family's budget, it can make the amount of life insurance cut in half because that person will not give up smoking. Many times, the non-smoking spouse would ask the smoking spouse if they would quit smoking. However, majority of the individuals that I met with would not give up smoking. I am not trying to judge smokers, but if it meant being able to afford the proper amount of life insurance for your family, it is something that you can detach from if you really want to.

As Christ Has

Jesus Christ gave the perfect example of how to deny yourself. Matthew 26:39 reads, *And he went a little farther, and fell on his face, and prayed, saying, O my Father, if it be possible, let this cup pass from me: nevertheless not as I will, but as thou wilt.* Jesus was in the Garden of Gethsemane preparing for his own crucifixion. Jesus had to deny himself because he did not want to take on this cup of suffering. He even prayed this a second time in verse 42: *He went away again the second time, and prayed, saying, O my Father, if this cup may not pass away from me, except I drink it, thy will be done.* This is the ultimate example of denying oneself.

Jesus also showed humility. Philippians 2:5-8 says, *⁵ Let this mind be in you, which was also in Christ Jesus: ⁶ Who, being in the form of God, thought it not robbery to be equal with God: ⁷ But made himself of no reputation, and took upon him the form of a servant, and was made in the likeness of men: ⁸ And being found in fashion as a man, he humbled himself, and became obedient unto death, even the death of the cross.* Verse 6 states that Jesus thought it was not robbery for him to be equal with God. When someone commits a robbery, they are taking something that does not belong to them. The first part of verse 6 explains that Jesus was in the form of God. Jesus is God! This is why it would be robbery for Jesus to be considered equal with God. However, as verse 7 states, he made himself of no reputation, took the form of a servant, and was made in man's likeness. Jesus was God coming to us on earth in human flesh. Verse 8 ends by stating that Jesus humbled himself and became obedient to death, even the death of the cross. If Jesus, being God, could humble himself, then we should be able to humble ourselves as well. Many times, people will not D.E.T.A.C.H. because of pride. Pride is the opposite of humility. As Proverbs 16:18 says, *Pride goeth before destruction, and an haughty spirit before a fall.* Don't let pride prevent you from D.E.T.A.C.H.ing. As I have heard a few pastors say, "You can either humble yourself or be humiliated." The difference is that humility is a choice that you make for yourself, but humiliation is someone else humbling you. Make your choice.

Sacrifice

Many times sacrifice is necessary to protect or preserve the future of yourself and/or loved ones. Many parents can relate to sacrificing for their children. You may not buy new clothes for yourself, so that your children can have new clothes. You may not be able to watch your favorite television programs, so that your kids can watch their cartoons. You may give up some of your hobbies, so that you can spend time with your children. Many parents sacrifice several things for their kids to have a better life.

People typically only sacrifice if they believe that what they are sacrificing for is worth it. God sacrificed Jesus because he thought you and I were worth it. You sacrifice various things for your kids or other relatives because you think they are worth it. Missionaries sacrifice their safety by going to many of the most dangerous places in the world because they believe that the gospel of Jesus Christ is worth it. If we need to sacrifice something to benefit the Kingdom of God, then I would hope that we would be willing to sacrifice it.

God sacrificed Jesus for us. John 3:16 reads, *For God so loved the world, that he gave his only begotten Son, that whosoever believeth in him should not perish, but have everlasting life.* God loves us so much that he sacrificed his only

Son, Jesus Christ for us. God did this because he wanted to offer us everlasting life. Jesus sacrificed temporarily on the cross on earth, so that we who believe in Him, have faith in Him, and follow Him can live eternally with Him in heaven. So the question we must ask ourselves is this: Is there ANYTHING that if God gave you a direct revelation to give it away, you could not trust Him and give it away? Is there ANYTHING that you will not detach from? Let's find out.

Chapter 3:
Examining Yourself

How do you find out what you are attached to and will not detach from? In order to find out, we must examine ourselves. There are three questions that we can ask ourselves to assist us in the process. 1) What do you spend a lot of time on? 2) What do you spend a lot of money on? 3) What makes you prideful?

Time

Time is such a valuable asset. Once you use it, you can't get it back. Whatever you spend time doing over the next 24 hours will become history. You will not be able to go back and change history. Therefore, how you spend your time is very important. It shows what you really value. You can spend your time doing just about anything. However, many of us spend our time on what we consider to be important.

Work is a great example. For many people, work is an area where they spend a great deal of time. I don't think there is anything wrong with working hard. However, working long hours starts to become a challenge and then a problem when you never see your family. If you are married, you should have a certain amount of time set aside to spend with your spouse. Also, if you have kids, you need to make time for them as well. Working to provide for your family is an awesome privilege. However, be aware that this does not give you a license to abandon family life. I understand that there are certain extremely busy seasons at work. For example, accountants typically have much longer working hours during tax season from about mid-January until April 15th. However, there should be some time in the following months for family time and relaxation. Or maybe, you just started a business. There are typically longer working hours when trying to get a business off the ground. However, when the business begins to stabilize some, you can carve out some time for family time, rest and relaxation. Is there anything that you spend too much time on that you need to detach from?

Money

Money is a very touchy subject for many people. Not many people want to share their personal finances. However, spending a lot of money in certain areas may reveal to you that there is an area that you need to detach from. What you spend money on shows what you value. I have heard people refer to the "checkbook test" many times. If you are not familiar with this, let me explain. If you will look at your checkbook or bank statement, you will be able to see the areas where you spend the most money. This is a good indicator that proves what you value. It also proves that sometimes, we don't put our money where our mouth is.

Professional sports are a great example. Let me start off by saying that I like sports. I really like sports. Professional football and basketball are my two favorites to watch. NFL (National Football League) season tickets can typically range from $400 to $4,000 or more for 8 home games and 2 preseason home games. NBA (National Basketball Association) season tickets can typically range from $500 up to $90,000 or more for 41 home games and 4 preseason home games. Some people can afford cheaper seats, and some can afford more expensive seats. The problem comes in when you buy tickets that cost more than your budget can handle. Also, you should compare what you are spending on season tickets to how much you are spending on other important things such as saving, giving, transportation or housing. Professional sports are a tough one because it can take a great deal of your time along with a great deal of money. I have nothing against professional sports, but athletes are generally paid a huge amount of money. The reason for this is that people continue to buy the tickets no matter the cost. This is the value that our society has placed on professional sports and professional athletes.

Pride

Pride has been the downfall of many people. We discussed pride in the last chapter when I stated that pride is the opposite of the humility that was modeled for us by Jesus. Pride is very dangerous.

Cars are a common example of how pride can lead to someone's downfall. Some individuals have a huge amount of pride in their cars. I believe many people will buy a car that they cannot afford before they buy a house that they cannot afford. I was once told, "If you want to see some nice cars, go take a look in the housing projects and lower income neighborhoods." For the most part, that guy was correct. There were Mercedes-Benz cars, BMW cars, Range Rovers, and many other more expensive cars. I am aware that some of them may have been drug dealers, but some of them were people who would rather save $300 a month by living in a dangerous housing project, so they could spend the extra $300 on a larger car payment. I have seen men, in many cases, have a classic car that they are restoring which becomes an obsession in their lives. They have always wanted that 1968 Shelby GT 500KR or that 1968 Dodge Charger R/T 440. Cars can take up a great deal of time and money, but the root of this problem many times is pride. If a man had one of these cars and they were having a very rough year financially, some of them would sell their house before they sold their classic car. This sounds crazy to some people, but this happens. They may even sell other essentials before selling their classic muscle car because they have so much pride wrapped up in owning that car. They want to show off their car to their buddies or they believe it is their status symbol. When anyone has this much pride in a car, they really need to D.E.T.A.C.H. Please don't misunderstand me here. There is nothing wrong with buying a classic car and/or restoring it. The issue is not with the car. The issue is the owner's heart and the amount of pride by placing the car above basic essentials. In some cases the car can become an idol, which is essentially placing it before God in our priority list.

Practical Example

One practical way to help you figure out if you are attached to something is to go down your personal balance sheet. I have included an example of a personal balance sheet for you if you are not familiar with one. There is an example of a personal balance sheet at the end of this chapter on page 51.

There is a blank copy of this form in the Appendix of this book for you to use. This is what you can use to determine your financial net worth. First, you list all of your assets, or everything you own that has value. Then, you list all of your liabilities, or everything that you owe money on. Afterwards, you subtract your liabilities from your assets. And yes, it is possible to have a negative net worth. That means that you owe more than you own. This may be an indication that there is something that you have not detached from.

To figure out if you are attached to something, just go down the list and ask yourself if God told me to give away _____ or get rid of _____, would I do it? If God told me to

D.E.T.A.C.H. Deny Earthly Things As Christ Has

give away my jewelry, would I do it? If God told me to sell my boat, would I do it? This exercise can be very helpful in determining whether or not you are truly detached from something. I want to be clear. This will be a difficult task to complete because it really challenges your heart.

You should now be able to answer these two questions. What are you ATTACHED to? What are you NOT willing to give up? Answering these questions honestly will lead to a proper examination of yourself.

Personal Balance Sheet *(Example)*

ASSETS (What You Own)	
Cash/Checking	$ 1,250
Savings	$ 3,500
Jewelry	$ 2,500
Furniture	$ 10,000
Retirement Accounts	$ 100,000
Investments	$ 50,000
Business Valuation (Current Value)	$ N/A
Automobiles/Boats	$ 45,000
Primary Home	$ 200,000
Other Real Estate	$ N/A
Other __Coin Collection__	$ 40,000
Other _____	$ N/A
TOTAL ASSETS	$ 452,250

LIABILITIES (What You Owe)	
Primary Home Mortgage	$ 150,000
Home Equity Line of Credit	$ 25,000
Other Real Estate Loans	$ N/A
Automobile/Boat Loans	$ 35,000
Student Loans	$ 30,000
Credit Card Debt	$ 10,000
Personal loans	$ 5,000
Business Loans	$ N/A
Other Loans __Furniture Loan__	$ 5,000
Other Debt _____	$ N/A
TOTAL LIABILITIES	$ 260,000
NET WORTH (total assets minus liabilities)	$ 192,250

Chapter 4:

Setting Priorities

Now that you have examined yourself and figured out what you need to detach from, you can start setting priorities. Setting priorities will allow you to determine what is first place in your life. If you are a Christian, God should be number one in your life. Whatever we give the highest priority to shows what is the most important to us. Our life and finances should reflect what we value. God should have first place in the area of our finances as well.

Seek God's Kingdom First

In Matthew chapter 6, there is a passage that shows us what our first priority should be. Verses 24 through 33 read, *[24] No man can serve two masters: for either he will hate the one, and love the other; or else he will hold to the one, and despise the other. Ye cannot serve God and mammon. [25] Therefore I say unto you, Take no thought for your life, what ye shall eat, or what ye shall drink; nor yet for your body, what ye shall put on. Is not the life more than meat, and the body than raiment? [26] Behold the fowls of the air: for they sow not, neither do they reap, nor gather into barns; yet your heavenly Father feedeth them. Are ye not much better than they? [27] Which of you by taking thought can add one cubit unto his stature? [28] And why take ye thought for raiment? Consider the lilies of the field, how they grow; they toil not, neither do they spin: [29] And yet I say unto you, That even Solomon in all his glory was not arrayed like one of these. [30] Wherefore, if God so clothe the grass of the field, which today is, and tomorrow is cast into the oven, shall he not much more clothe you,*

O ye of little faith? ³¹ Therefore take no thought, saying, What shall we eat? or, What shall we drink? or, Wherewithal shall we be clothed? ³² (For after all these things do the Gentiles seek:) for your heavenly Father knoweth that ye have need of all these things. ³³ But seek ye first the kingdom of God, and his righteousness; and all these things shall be added unto you.

Let's break this passage down. Verse 24 is stating that we cannot serve two masters, God and mammon. You have to pick one. Mammon can be defined as money, riches, greed, material wealth, and/or possessions that a person trusts in. So you cannot serve God and mammon at the same time. Only one can be the priority. Verses 25-30 state that you should take no thought for your life about what you will eat, what you will drink, and what you will wear. Take no thought can be translated to do not worry. In other words do not worry about what you will eat, drink or wear. Verse 31 restates this by stating again that you should take no thought or don't worry about what you will eat, what you will drink, or what you will wear. Then verse 32 states why, when it says that the Gentiles seek after all "these things." Gentiles are pagans or heathens. These people are not followers of Jesus. Therefore, we should not be prioritizing the same things that the Gentiles are prioritizing. Verse 32 then finishes by declaring that your heavenly father knows that you need "these things." God knows all of your needs already. Verse 33 finishes this passage with, *But seek ye first the kingdom of God, and his righteousness; and all these things shall be added unto you.* To seek *first* the kingdom of God means to give it the highest priority. It is saying that nothing else is more important than the kingdom of God. Then, all of "these things" will be added unto you. "These things" are referred to twice in this passage. "These things" are your food, drink and clothing as is states for the second time at the end of verse 31 leading into verse 32. In other words "these things" are your needs. God may provide some of your wants, but this passage is referring to your needs. The promise here is that if we keep God first place in our lives, he will provide all of our needs.

Setting Priorities

A Matter of the Heart

Our heart needs to be focused on the Lord. Matthew 6:21 says, *For where your treasure is, there will your heart be also.* Your treasure does not follow your heart. Your heart follows your treasure. Review each category on your spending plan or budget. If the majority of your finances are spent on entertainment, then that is where your heart is. If the majority of your finances are spent on food, then that is where your heart is. If the majority of your finances are spent on your car, then that is where your heart is. Also, if the majority of your finances are spent giving generously to the work of the Lord, then that is where your heart is.

Also, the Bible says in Proverbs 4:23, *Keep thy heart with all diligence; for out of it are the issues of life.* Another way to say keep your heart is to guard your heart or watch over your heart. If your heart follows your treasure and the issues of life come from your heart, then it is very important to take note of where your treasure or finances are. Your heart will follow your finances, money, possessions, or "treasure," and will impact the issues of your life. In essence, your "treasure," including your money, possessions, and finances, will definitely impact the issues of life. Nobody can deny that money and finances touch many areas of your life. What we do with our finances affects where we live, what we eat, what we drive, what we wear and more. But even more basic, it affects whether or not we have a place to live, whether or not we can buy food to eat, and whether or not we have a car to drive. How you manage your personal finances will determine where your heart is and how you react to the issues of life.

First, Really?

In Luke chapter 9, Jesus really spells out what it means to put God's kingdom first. Verses 57-62 read, *⁵⁷And it came to pass, that, as they went in the way, a certain man said unto him, Lord, I will follow thee whithersoever thou goest. ⁵⁸And Jesus said unto him, Foxes have holes, and birds of the air have nests; but the Son of man hath not where to lay his head. ⁵⁹And he said unto another, Follow me. But he said, Lord,*

Setting Priorities

suffer me first to go and bury my father. ⁶⁰ Jesus said unto him, Let the dead bury their dead: but go thou and preach the kingdom of God. ⁶¹ And another also said, Lord, I will follow thee; but let me first go bid them farewell, which are at home at my house.⁶² And Jesus said unto him, No man, having put his hand to the plough, and looking back, is fit for the kingdom of God.

Let's discuss this passage. In verse 57, a man comes up to Jesus and says that he wants to follow him wherever he goes. Jesus responds in verse 58 by stating that he has no place to lay his head. This lets us know that there is a cost to following Jesus. Verse 59 continues with Jesus telling a different man to follow him. This man responds by asking Jesus if he could *first* go and bury his father. The man was putting his father's burial in first place. Jesus responds in verse 60 by telling the man to let the dead bury their dead, but go and preach the kingdom of God. Jesus was telling him to put the kingdom of God *first*. In verse 61, a different man tells Jesus that he will follow him but he wants to say farewell and goodbye to his family *first*. Jesus concludes this passage in verse 32 by stating that no man who puts his hand to the plow and looks back is fit for the kingdom of God. These are very challenging words. You would think that the things that these men want to do are honorable. There is generally nothing wrong with burying your dead father or saying farewell and goodbye to your family at home. So why did Jesus have a problem with this? It was because they wanted to do those things *first*. Jesus is very clear again stating that the kingdom of God must be *first*.

Do you find yourself thinking about certain things that you are inclined to do *first*? Do you ever think things this? *First,* let me succeed at this business and then I will follow God's call to ministry. *First*, let me achieve millionaire status and then I will follow Jesus. *First*, let my children finish college and then I will be a generous giver. *First*, let me buy my dream home and then I will trust God. Is God REALLY first place in every area of your life, including your finances? If not, decide NOW to make him *first* place.

Chapter 5:
Determining to Free Yourself

Debt is a huge problem in our society today. I define debt as something that you owe, usually money, that you are obligated to pay back. Over the last 8 years as a financial professional and currently a Biblical financial teacher, I have met with hundreds of individuals and families. They have come to me for advice on many different topics: saving, budgeting, insurance, retirement, stewardship and more. I have done many one-on-one coaching sessions with these individuals and families. About 99% of the time, the main problem people have is debt. I get to see firsthand how debt affects individuals and families. This is why I strongly discourage people from getting into debt. Let's discuss the effects of debt.

Slavery

Proverbs 22:7 says, *The rich ruleth over the poor, and the borrower is servant to the lender.* The New International Version (NIV) translates servant as slave. So it reads: *The rich rule over the poor, and the borrower is **slave** to the lender* [emphasis mine]. The Bible describes debt as financial slavery. The borrower is always slave to the lender, no matter who the lender is. The lender can be a bank, a mortgage company, credit card companies, friends or even family members. When you borrow money, you always create the lender and slave relationship. I remember when I was in college and I started a business. I borrowed some money from my sister for startup capital. Do you want to guess what happened to our relationship? It was strained badly! I did not want to be around her, even at family functions. This is because I was feeling like a slave. I was a slave to the lender, my sister. In my mind, it did not matter that we were related. It did not matter that she was willing to lend me the money. I was a borrower and I felt the bondage and slavery of the debt that I owed to her. Then, a few weeks or so later, I saw her at my mother's house. She looked at me and said that we needed to discuss some payment terms. I knew at that moment that it was time to pay her back as soon as possible. I paid her back the next week! Boy was I ecstatic when I walked up to her door and paid her back all at once, in full, with cash money and with 10% interest. I learned that day that the borrower is truly slave to the lender in all circumstances.

Many people would like to debate about debt and classify good debt verses bad debt, but I think all debt is bad debt. We should not be a slave to any person or lender in this world. There is something very interesting at the end of Proverbs 22:7. It's a PERIOD! This scripture does not say the borrower is slave to the lender *except* on a car. This scripture does not say the borrower is slave to the lender *except* on a business. This scripture does not say the borrower is slave to the lender *except* on a mortgage. This scripture does not say the borrower is slave to the lender *except* on a student loan. It says the borrower is slave to the lender – PERIOD. If there were no credit cards or car loans available, people would be FORCED to live within their means! You would not see as many brand new cars on the road, and many would not take extravagant vacations and buy as many expensive clothes, if the credit was not available to them. Let's not put a question mark where God's word has put a period. Now, let's examine some of the root causes and reasons why people get into debt.

What is the Root Cause?

Usually debt is just an indication that there is a root cause somewhere that convinced someone to borrow money. Sometimes debt is simply caused by financial illiteracy or ignorance. However, many times there is a root cause. Let's address 6 common root causes of debt: impatience, lack of trust, medical expenses, divorce, envy and addictions.

First, let's discuss impatience. We live in a society where we want everything now. Unfortunately, many people can have it now because lenders are allowing it. One example

Determining to Free Yourself

---

is interest-free financing. There are a lot of "0% interest for 90 days" advertisements. Well, I want to tell you to read the fine print of the offer. There is typically a high interest rate that applies if you make only one mistake or if you are only one day late. Why not just save for 3 months and pay cash? That's because many of the people want it NOW. Furniture stores are notorious for this as well. Many times you see an advertisement in a sales paper that says "No Interest Until 2020," in big letters. Many people don't realize all of the terms that apply to the "No Interest Until 2020" financing offers. There are several details in the small print that you may not realize. For example, the actual interest rate is usually between 28 and 29 percent. In many of these financing offers, if you don't pay the entire balance in full by the end of the promotional period, you end up paying the 28 or 29 percent interest rate retroactively all the way back to your initial purchase date. Also, in many plans, if you miss one payment or pay late one time, then you have to start paying interest at the 28 or 29 percent interest rate retroactively all the way back to your initial purchase date. These stores and financing companies realize that many of the people who sign up for these financing plans will not pay the balance in full, they will miss a payment, or make at least one late payment. This allows the finance company to collect that high interest rate, usually 28 or 29 percent, for the entire period back to the date that you originally made the purchase. Don't let impatience get you into debt.

Next, a lack of trust sometimes contributes to someone going into debt. When God gives you a promise, you can trust Him. I have heard countless stories of people who were about to borrow money on something such as a car. Then, the Holy Spirit spoke to them and told them to wait. Finally, a month or so later, someone gave them a car or gave them the money to buy one. Borrowing money can deny God the opportunity to provide for you in miraculous ways.

Medical Expenses are also a common cause of debt. Currently, medical expenses are actually the number one cause of bankruptcy. Many of the major medical expenses you have may come as a surprise. You don't know in advance if your health will suddenly change. This is why it is important to be prepared by purchasing health insurance. Even if you don't like going to the doctor or if you don't plan on going to the doctor, you should get what I call an "emergency policy." This is just purchasing the cheapest policy with the highest deductible, for example a $10,000 deductible. This means that if you have an emergency surgery, or some other expensive covered medical expense, you won't have to pay more than $10,000. Let me give you an example of why health insurance is important. I know a young man in his 20s who suddenly came down with leukemia. He had a wife and a child at this point as well. However, he did not have health insurance. He told me that over a 6 month period, he received about $100,000 in medical bills. My heart was broken for him and his young family. If he would have had even a high deductible health insurance plan with a $10,000 deductible, it would have changed the situation dramatically. His medical bills would have maxed out at $10,000 instead of having $100,000 in medical bills. I'm sure anyone would rather pay $10,000 in medical bills than $100,000. Having to fight leukemia is hard enough, but to worry about finances makes it much more difficult. Don't let

D.E.T.A.C.H. Deny Earthly Things As Christ Has

unexpected medical expenses ruin your finances. Purchase some form of health insurance.

Divorce is a very tragic event. According to numerous surveys and statistics, the number one cause of divorce is money fights. Managing finances God's way is very important in a marriage. When divorce does occur, both spouses are usually left in undesirable financial circumstances. Suddenly, both spouses have to move out and pay all of their own separate bills. Each has to pay their own rent or mortgage, utilities, food, internet and so on. Thus, they may end up borrowing money to try to maintain the same lifestyle as when they were married. If both spouses were working outside the home, the spouse with the lower income may suffer worse. A high percentage of my one-on-one financial coaching time goes to single moms. Some of these cases are because of divorce. Many single moms may borrow money to keep their children living the same lifestyle as they were before the divorce, even if the single mom makes much less money. This can lead to a very large debt load. I have a heart that has a soft spot for single moms because my mom is a single mom due to my father having a heart attack when I was 21 years old. In general, single moms do have tough financial situations. If you are a single mom reading this book, I want to encourage you to press on and eliminate debt as best as you can. Please do not feel guilty if your children have to lower their lifestyle for a few years while you are getting out debt.

Another common cause of debt is envy. Envy is simply wanting what someone else has. Some may even go to the extent of harming someone else to get what they want. Many people have heard of the phrase "Keeping up with the Joneses." This is when someone wants to have the same or a better version of their friend's or neighbor's possessions. They want the same size house or a bigger house. They want the same car or a better and more expensive car. This is an easy way to find yourself buried in debt. Trying to keep up with other people is not worth it. You don't have to compare your possessions and status with everyone else's. Comparing your possessions with others is a recipe for disaster. Envy has been the downfall of many people including lower, middle and upper class people and has caused them to go deep into debt.

Lastly, addictions are a common cause of debt. When someone has an addiction they will do just about anything to "get their fix." Addictions can be many things. They can be drugs, alcohol, gambling, pornography or other things. Addictions can be hard to catch. For example, if your spouse has an addiction, they may do their best to hide it from you as long as possible. They might take out a credit card without you knowing, open a separate bank account, or lie about where they are going. The person with the addiction is usually ashamed, so they do not want you to find out. Therefore, they will do almost anything to hide it from you.

These are 6 of the common root causes of debt. Some of these may need to be broken down further. They may result from childhood circumstances or lifelong desires. In any case, you have to dig as deep as necessary to figure what the root is, so that once the individual or couple gets out of debt, they will not end up going back into debt. If you have any debt, can you identify with any of these root causes? If not, can you think of a different root cause that may have caused you to go into debt?

Opportunity Cost

Opportunity cost must be considered when you are making debt payments. Many people do not realize this. When you spend money paying debt, you lose the opportunity to use that money for something else. The money that you use to pay your car payment cannot be used to give. The money you spend paying credit card companies cannot be used to save or invest. Let me give you an example. Suppose you wanted to save for your child to go to college. However, you felt that you could not save because you were paying $200 per month on your credit cards. If you didn't have that credit card debt and invested $200 per month at 8% for 18 years, then you would have over $96,000 saved up for your kid's college. You lost out on the opportunity to save almost $100,000 for your kid's college because you spent it every month paying credit cards and the accompanying interest. Another example could be that you want to give more to your church, a Christian ministry or a Christian missionary. Think about the eternal and spiritual impact your giving would have in these places that build the kingdom of God. Someone coming to faith in Christ is PRICELESS! You should always consider that paying debt not only costs you more in interest, it may also prevent you from being a generous giver and/or saving for your family's future. Look over your current debts and your monthly debt payments. What opportunity or opportunities are these debt payments preventing you from participating in?

Wicked?

If we want to know what God thinks about us repaying our debts, then we should look to the Bible for answers. God is very clear in His Word about us repaying our debts. One scripture, Psalm 37:21 says, *The wicked borrow and do not repay, but the righteous give generously.* (NIV) The first part of this verse, says the wicked borrow and do not repay. By not honoring our word and paying our debts, we show traits of wickedness. When we see or hear the word wicked, we think of violent crimes, drugs, alcohol and other things. However, not paying your debts is not something many people would describe as wicked. We should do our best to repay all of our debts including loans, credit cards, material items or anything that we owe. I am not completely ruling out bankruptcy, because some people have gotten so far into debt it may be almost impossible to get out of debt based on their income. However, I do not believe that everyone who files bankruptcy is actually bankrupt. As a follower of Christ, we should give every effort to repay all of our debts. If a creditor sues you, and forces you into bankruptcy, then you may not have an option. Do the best that you can with what you have. By striving to repay all that you owe, you are not showing any traits of wickedness. Pray to God to show you how to manage the money you have as best as possible.

A Blessing

Deuteronomy chapter 28 is known by many as the blessings and curses chapter. The first 14 verses list the blessings for obedience. Verse 12 states, ...*thou shalt lend unto many nations, and thou shalt not borrow.* The scripture says *thou shalt **not** borrow* [emphasis mine]. This is similar to the situation in Proverbs 22:7. It does not say, thou shalt not borrow *except* for a car, or *except* for a student loan, or *except* for a business. This scripture is stating that not borrowing money is a blessing. Why would being debt free be a blessing? Being debt free is a blessing because you free yourself financially to do whatever God calls you to do. Many times, people use a lack of finances as an excuse to not follow through with something that God has called them to do. When you pay off all of your debts, your personal finances change from being an excuse to being a blessing.

Proverbs 10:22 says, *The blessing of the LORD, it maketh rich, and he addeth no sorrow with it.* When God blesses you, there will be no sorrow added to it. Just imagine that today is your birthday. You are having a birthday party at your house and your closest relative comes in. Then, your relative tells you that they have a surprise for you. It is a very expensive gift. However, you first have to put on a blindfold. You agree to being blindfolded and you get very excited. Your relative walks you outside and you get even more excited. This must be something big! Now, your relative takes the blindfold off of your face. It's a brand new Mercedes-Benz automobile with a big red bow on the front of it! Wow! What a present! You scream, jump up and down, and run around the car. You are ecstatic! Your relative gives you the keys. You open the door and wait...there is a paper on the seat? You read it and find out that it is a finance agreement. This car comes with a $750 car payment for 72 months. Yikes! Your relative smiles and says that they got you a good "deal" with 0% interest financing. Well, thanks to an earlier part of this chapter, you know where I stand on the issue of "no interest financing." Now that car payment is sorrow that is added to this so called "blessing." You can leave your imagination now. When God blesses you, you don't have to worry about any added sorrow. In this example, a blessing of God would have been different. There would not have been a car payment to go along with the car. God would have provided a blessing without the added sorrow.

D.E.T.A.C.H. Deny Earthly Things As Christ Has

Debt Snowball

Let me give you some guidance on how to get out of debt. There are 2 basic methods to paying off your debts: highest interest rate and the debt snowball. The highest interest rate method suggests that you pay off the debt with the highest interest rate first, regardless of the balance. This method is the fastest way to pay off your debts mathematically. However, I believe in behavioral finance, which suggests the debt snowball method. With the debt snowball, you pay off your debts from smallest to largest. You pay minimum payments on all debts except the smallest one. Add all extra money to the smallest debt. When you pay it off, you add that amount to the next smallest debt and so on until you have paid all debts. As you pay off a small debt quickly, you get a quick victory. You begin to get more and more motivated to pay off your debt as quickly as possible. For example, you had 6 debts last month, but 2 months later you only have 5 debts left. Then, 4 months later, you only have 4 debts left. This method creates a lot of focus, passion and intensity, which will be needed to get out of debt quickly. Here is an example of a debt snowball:

Determining to Free Yourself

Debt Snowball *(Example)*				
Item	Balance	Minimum Payment	Total Payment	Interest Rate
Visa credit card	$300.00	$20.00	$120.00	20.9%
Discover credit card	$800.00	$35.00	$35.00	15.0%
MasterCard credit card	$2,500	$105.00	$105.00	29.9%
Car Loan	$18,500	$300.00	$300.00	7.0%
Student Loan #1	$22,000	$260.00	$260.00	6.8%
TOTAL	$44,100	$720.00	$820.00	N/A

Instructions: List your debts smallest to largest. Pay minimum payments on all debts except the smallest one. Add all extra money to the smallest debt. When you pay it off, you add that amount to the next smallest debt and so on until you have paid all debts.

In this example, the person is paying the minimum payment on all debts except the smallest one. This person is adding $100 per month extra to the $20 minimum payment and will be paying Visa $120 per month. After a few months, the Visa credit card will be paid off. When the Visa credit card is paid off, this person will add that $120 per month to the Discover credit card and will begin paying Discover $120 plus the minimum $35 to equal $155 per month until it is paid off and so on. The quick victories from paying the Visa and Discover credit cards off in a relatively short period will help motivate this person to continue to pay off debt as quickly as possible. If this person would have chosen the highest interest method, they would have ended up paying the MasterCard first, taking over a year to pay off the first credit card. That can be discouraging when starting to pay off debt. This is why I agree with behavioral finance and recommend the debt snowball approach. There is a blank debt snowball form in the Appendix of this book for you to use.

In this chapter we have discussed biblical reasons and practical reasons to get out of debt and avoid debt in the future. I have seen what debt can do and has done to many individuals and families. College students have committed suicide after racking up credit card debt. Married couples have divorced. Missionaries have been prevented from fulfilling the great commission overseas in many nations around the world. Being loaded with debt has a devastating impact on anyone. I believe I have made myself very clear. I believe I have made what God's word says about debt very clear. I hope I have convinced you to determine to free yourself from debt. Make the decision now to free yourself from financial slavery! GET OUT OF DEBT!!!

Chapter 6:
Practicing Contentment

The Merriam-Webster dictionary defines content as "pleased and satisfied; not needing more." Therefore, contentment is when you can be happy and satisfied without needing more. This is a very difficult thing to attain in today's society because of how often we are marketed to. Let's start with a foundational truth that can help us to become content.

God Owns It All

The foundation of understanding biblical personal finance lies in this statement, "God owns it all." Psalm 24:1 says, *The earth is the Lord's, and everything in it, the world, and all who live in it.* (NIV) Also, Psalm 50:10-12 says, *for every animal of the forest is mine, and the cattle on a thousand hills. I know every bird in the mountains, and the insects in the fields are mine. If I were hungry I would not tell you, for the world is mine, and all that is in it.* (NIV) These verses express to us that God owns it all. So if he owns everything, then we are stewards or managers and not owners. The steward in the Bible was the person who managed the financial affairs of someone else. This is our position today as we manage the money and possessions that God owns and has entrusted to us. This is contrary to our culture today. The American dream is based on what we "own,"- a home, a car, a business or other material possessions. We must mentally make a shift in our thinking to help us understand that we are not owners, but stewards. Many times we use the word "stewardship" or "stewardship campaign" in our churches today when talking about giving only. However, stewardship is more than just giving. Stewardship includes how we manage the entire 100% of our income and possessions. When you truly understand

and realize that God owns it all, contentment will be easier to attain.

I remember attending a Christian business luncheon one Wednesday. A guy got up to share his testimony with us. He was a "Brother" associated with the Brothers of the Christian schools. He was currently the President of one of their high schools in Louisiana. There was one statement that he said which spoke volumes to me. He said, "I do not own anything in my name and that keeps my perspective right." He did not own anything, LITERALLY. I began to think about that. This is how we should think when it comes to money and possessions. So what if the bank calls you a "homeowner" even when you still owe money on the home. So what if the car dealership says that you "own" a car, even though you put no money down and have 6 years of car payments left. In reality, we need to keep our minds and thoughts focused on this fact: God owns it all and we are His stewards or financial managers.

What Does Someone Need to Be Content?

Why is it so hard to be content? The answer to this question is based on your perspective. Many people think that in order to be content, they "need" to have a new car, a $300,000 house, and an annual income of at least $100,000. Some would say that is fair. Some would say that is too little. Some would say that they can be content with a little less than that. Let's take a look at the Bible and see what the Apostle Paul wrote in 1 Timothy. 1 Timothy 6:6-8 reads, *But godliness with contentment is great gain. ⁷ For we brought nothing into the world, and we can take nothing out of it. ⁸ But if we have food and clothing, we will be content with that.* (NIV) The Bible tells us that we only need two things for contentment: food and clothing. This is a very challenging statement! This is also not specific to a certain type of food or clothing. The scripture does not say if we have lobster, steak and caviar for food, we will be content. The scripture does not say if we have Armani, Dolce & Gabbana and Prada, we will be content. The scripture says simply food and clothing. Therefore, if you have any type of food to eat and any type of clothing to wear, then you can be content.

I was once asked in one of the classes that I was teaching, "Should a homeless person be content with food and clothing?" I responded with this, "Contentment does not mean that you give up or stop working hard toward goals. It just means that your happiness and satisfaction do not depend on getting more and more." Getting more "stuff," achieving more accomplishments, or gaining more recognition are not prerequisites to contentment. Contentment does not mean settling, it just means that your attitude changes.

Attitude

Attitude is a very important factor in developing a biblical mindset for personal finance. God knows what we are really thinking on the inside. We can't fake it with Him. 1 Timothy 6:9-10, reads, *But they that will be rich fall into temptation and a snare, and into many foolish and hurtful lusts, which drown men in destruction and perdition. [10] For the love of money is the root of all evil: which while some coveted after, they have erred from the faith, and pierced themselves through with many sorrows.* Many times, I ask people if money is the root of all evil. The majority of the time, people answer yes. However, that is incorrect. The Bible says that the *love* of money is the root of all evil. This deals with our heart and our attitude. Money by itself has no morals. It is the morals of the person who possesses it that makes it used for evil or for good. Falling in love with money makes you susceptible to err from the faith or be led astray. 1 John 2:15 says, *Love not the world, neither the things that are in the world. If any man love the world, the love of the Father is not in him.* There is that word love again. Love is an emotion that does not need to be caught up in worldly things. Loving the world or the things of the world is a trap that leads to many sorrows and disappointments. Here is the truth. Once you are truly content, wealth and riches will not destroy you. Lottery winners going broke, being addicted to drugs, or going to jail within a few years are examples of riches destroying someone who did not have the correct attitude or character to handle great wealth. If you will develop a truly biblical attitude toward money and possessions, then you will be able to be materially wealthy and still be an exemplary follower of Jesus.

Contentment Must Be Learned

I have not made light of the difficulty of contentment. I continue to point out that it is not easy to be content. It is actually quite challenging. In the Bible, the Apostle Paul speaks of contentment again in the book of Philippians. Philippians 4:11-12 reads, *...for I have learned to be content whatever the circumstances. ¹² I know what it is to be in need, and I know what it is to have plenty. I have learned the secret of being content in any and every situation, whether well fed or hungry, whether living in plenty or in want.*" (NIV) Paul is stating that he had to *learn* to be content. It wasn't easy. It did not come to him naturally. That is the same situation with us. We must *learn* to be content. It is hard to be content when we have marketing emails that we receive before we even wake up. We hear advertisements on the radio on the way to work. We pass by billboard signs with advertisements. When we watch television, we have commercials that come on trying to sell us something. However, the reality is that these products will not make us happy in the long term. Then, Paul states *"in any and every situation."* What is excluded in that statement? Nothing! I understand that we all have different situations, but we have to learn contentment no matter what situation we find ourselves in. These are more challenging verses from the Apostle Paul. We shouldn't believe only part of the scriptures. We should believe all of the scriptures.

People who say or think things like "I will be happy when..." or "I won't be happy until..."are not content. Many people say, "I will be happy when my income reaches over $100,000 a year." Many people say, "I will be happy when I buy a home." Some say, "I won't be happy until I get a new car." Some say, "I won't be happy until I become famous." These things are not bad in themselves. It is just the attitude of "I will be happy when..." or "I won't be happy until..." that make these people discontent. When these two statements are completely removed from your vocabulary, it is a sign that you are probably on your way to being content.

Chapter 7:
Living for God's Kingdom

When developing a biblical mindset for personal finance, we should understand that we are living for God's kingdom. There should be a balance between many things. I have broken it down into the following four areas: saving, serving, giving and eternal perspective. A proper balance of these four areas will help you live for God's kingdom. Let's start with saving.

Saving

Because this book is titled, "D.E.T.A.C.H. – Deny Earthly Things As Christ Has," many individuals may wonder if I believe that you should not save money. This is NOT what I am saying. Saving money is an important part of personal finance. Sometimes, when I teach biblical financial stewardship, a participant may ask, "If God owns it all, then why do I need to save money? He will just give me everything I need." This is partially true in the sense that God does own it all and he can do whatever he wants. However, God does tell us in His Word that we should save for the future. Proverbs 21:20 says, *There is treasure to be desired and oil in the dwelling of the wise; but a foolish man spendeth it up.* This verse tells us that foolish people spend everything that they make. According to the American Payroll Association, almost 70 percent of Americans are living paycheck to paycheck.[1] Also, a recent survey shows that over one-third of workers have less than $1,000 saved for retirement.[2] This is NOT Kingdom Living. Kingdom Living does not mean that you don't save money. It just means that you save with a biblical attitude. We just learned about having a biblical attitude in the last chapter. We just need to determine our motive when saving. Are you saving to provide for your family? Are you saving just to be rich? If you are honest with yourself, have you fallen in love with money? Nevertheless, saving is necessary.

There are 3 basic reasons why you should save money. First, you should save for emergencies. Proverbs 6:6-8 says, *Go to the ant, you sluggard; consider its ways and be wise! It has no commander, no overseer or ruler, yet it stores its provisions in summer and gathers its food at harvest.* (NIV) These verses teach us that even an ant is smart enough to store up for "winter" or emergencies and hard times. Have you ever had a flat tire on your car? Has your cell phone ever had water damage? Have you had any unexpected medical bills? Has your refrigerator ever needed fixing? All of these things are emergencies, but it helps to have the money saved up to pay cash for these emergency situations. Next, you should save for large purchases. This is how you pay cash for your car, TV, sofa, or new business. When you save for large purchases, you prevent yourself from going into debt. Lastly, you should save for long term planning including retirement and your children's college. Some people tell me that they do not plan to retire so they do not feel the need to save for retirement.

There is nothing wrong with working full-time for your entire life. However, how do you know that your health will be the same in your 70s as it was in your 50s? How do you know that you won't have to change your work schedule to take care of a parent or family member? Why not work because you want to and not because you have to? When it comes to college planning for your children, it is such a blessing for them to go to college and graduate debt-free. When you save and plan for this expense, it prevents you and/or your children from going into student loan debt. If they end up not attending college or receive a full scholarship, you can help them with these finances in some other way.

Serving

Serving is an awesome privilege. Some people serve on a regular basis and experience much joy. Some people simply don't want to serve, and others don't see the need to serve just as I didn't see the need to serve for many years. However, when you give your time and talents to expand the kingdom of God, you are becoming more like Jesus. Matthew 20:26-28 reads, *...Instead, whoever wants to become great among you must be your servant, [27] and whoever wants to be first among you must be your slave-[28] just as the Son of Man did not come to be served, but to serve, and to give his life as a ransom for many.* (NIV) According to these scripture verses, serving is very significant in the kingdom of God. Even Jesus came, not to be served, but to serve.

I used to be like the individuals who didn't see the need to serve. I just went to church on Sunday and went home without really serving anyone throughout the entire week. After I began to serve, I began to experience the joy of the Lord like never before! Over the last several years, I have served in homeless ministry on Saturday mornings at least once every month. More of my time during other times of the week has been spent serving and discipling others. At my church, I serve by ushering and any other area that they need volunteers. I am not telling you these things to brag on myself. I am telling you these things because I have realized how much joy I receive while I am serving. This is something you will not experience until you do it for yourself. Let me encourage you to start serving in some way. Pray to God about where he wants you to serve.

Giving

Giving is a very popular topic when it comes to finance in the church. I believe giving is very important. In this section, I am specifically speaking about giving financially. I referred to giving of your time and talents in the serving section. The first thing that I would like to discuss is tithing. Sometimes, people incorrectly use the word tithe. They say, "I give a 5% tithe." Or "I give a 7% tithe." However, the word tithe literally means giving "one-tenth" or 10% of your income. Saying that you give a 7% tithe is like saying that you give a 70 cent dollar. A dollar is 100 cents, not 70 cents. Oftentimes, individuals will try to put a ceiling or floor on the tithe. For example, let's say that one person makes $100,000 per year and gives $10,000 to their local church as their 10% tithe. Another person makes $30,000 per year and gives $3,000 to their local church as their 10% tithe. Some people would say that the person that gave $10,000 gave more. Others would say that the person that gave $3,000 gave more because their budget is smaller and they probably had to sacrifice more. However, both of these statements are incorrect. These two people gave the same amount. Why? Because it is a percentage. Tithing is the same regardless of the amount of money you make. There is no ceiling or floor. Keep this in mind whenever you discuss tithing.

Let's take a look at what the Bible says about tithing. Malachi 3:8-10 says, *"Will a mere mortal rob God? Yet you rob me. But you ask, 'How are we robbing you?' In tithes and offerings. ⁹ You are under a curse—your whole nation—because you are robbing me. ¹⁰ Bring the whole tithe into the storehouse, that there may be food in my house. Test me in this," says the LORD Almighty, "and see if I will not throw open the floodgates of heaven and pour out so much blessing that there will not be room enough to store it."* (NIV) These verses clearly state that God telling us to tithe. This is also the only place in the Bible that God says to test Him. By far, the most common objection to this is that it is in the Old Testament. However, tithing is mentioned multiple times in the New Testament as well. Jesus says in Matthew 23:23, *Woe unto you, scribes and Pharisees, hypocrites! for ye pay tithe of mint and anise and cummin, and have omitted the weightier matters of the law, judgment, mercy, and faith: these ought ye to have done, and not to leave the other undone.* Jesus is stating that you ought to tithe. This is JESUS saying this! This is not Jonathan Sayles saying this. Jesus is saying that you should tithe. If that doesn't convince you, then I don't know what will.

I began to think about what would happen if every Christian tithed. I came across an article that stated that there would be an additional $165 billion for churches to use and allocate, if every Christian gave 10 percent of their income.[3] WOW! That's a lot of money! The church could do many great things for God's kingdom, if every Christian decided to tithe. Tithing is just the starting place for giving.

Generous giving goes beyond tithing. I believe that generosity doesn't start until your giving reaches 11%. In my opinion, everything above the tithe is what can be considered as generosity. Many times we see an athlete give $100,000 and we think they are generous. However, you go back and see that this athlete made $10 million dollars that year. This means that the $100,000 donation is only 1% of their income. If they are tithing by giving 10% to their church, AND giving this to a charity, then it is generous. On the other hand, if this is the only giving that they are doing, then I would not consider it generous.

One popular scripture on giving is Luke 6:38, which reads, *Give, and it will be given to you. A good measure, pressed down, shaken together and running over, will be poured into your lap. For with the measure you use, it will be measured to you.* (NIV) This verse is actually the same passage as Matthew 7 verses 1 and 2, which refer to judging others. It really is referring to the principle of sowing and reaping. You will reap whatever you sow. If you sow judgment, you will reap judgment. However, this does apply to finances as well. I experienced this when we were starting our ministry, Kingdom Financial Education. There was a missionary that the Lord kept putting on my heart to support financially. My wife and I decided to support him with a $1,000 donation. About a month later, I went to check our post office box. On that same day, I had a receipt for the $1,000 donation that we sent to the missionary in one hand, and a $1,000 donation check from a church that decided to support our ministry in the other hand. We have actually received more from that church since then, but I believe that the Lord honored our trust in Him at a time when we could have used that money to help us start this brand new ministry from scratch. Let me make a HUGE DISCLAIMER here! I am not saying that if you give $1,000 today, then you will receive a $1,000 the next month and more just like my wife and I did. God works with each person and situation as He decides. I do believe you will reap what you sow; however, I do not know the timeframe or the method that God will use. Let me challenge you to at least begin tithing. If you are already tithing, let me encourage you to give over and above your tithes to support the work of the Lord. You can do this by giving to a missionary, Christian ministry, or a special church project or fund. Become a generous giver and experience what Jesus said in Acts 20:35, ...*It is more blessed to give than to receive.* This too, is something I can't explain with just words. This is something you will not experience until you do it for yourself.

Also, when we become a giver, we take on one of God's characteristics. John 3:16 reads, *For God so loved the world, that he **gave** his only begotten Son, that whosoever believeth in him should not perish, but have everlasting life.* [emphasis mine] God is a giver. He gave up His only Son, Jesus Christ, to die on the cross to pay the penalty for our sins. When we become generous givers, we are following God's example.

Eternal Perspective

When developing a biblical mindset for personal finance, it is essential to have an eternal perspective. This eternal perspective really brings this entire book and D.E.T.A.C.H. concept together. This is what happened to me during my Mission trip to Reynosa, Mexico, as I shared with you in Chapter 1. My PERSPECTIVE had changed!

Why should we deny earthly things as Christ has? Because at the end of our lives, eternity is what matters. 2 Corinthians 4:18 reads, *While we look not at the things which are seen, but at the things which are not seen: for the things which are seen are temporal; but the things which are not seen are eternal.* Anything on this earth that we physically see is only temporary. The Apostle Paul tells us in this scripture that these are not the things to look at or focus on. Paul tells us to look at or focus on the things that are not seen. The things that we cannot see are the things that will last forever. When someone buys an expensive car or home, it will only last temporarily. However, when someone comes to faith in Jesus Christ and becomes His follower, that decision changes their eternal future and destines them for Heaven. Heaven will last for eternity.

Following the love of money scripture in 1 Timothy 6:10, the Apostle Paul writes in 1 Timothy 6:11-12, *But thou, O man of God, flee these things; and follow after righteousness, godliness, faith, love, patience, meekness. [12] Fight the good fight of faith, lay hold on eternal life, whereunto thou art also called, and hast professed a good profession before many witnesses.* Paul is telling us to flee the temptation of falling in love with money and follow after righteousness, godliness, faith, love, patience and meekness. He tells us to lay hold on eternal life, which is where our attention should be. Later in the same chapter, the Apostle Paul writes in 1 Timothy 6:17-19, *Charge them that are rich in this world, that they be not highminded, nor trust in uncertain riches, but in the living God, who giveth us richly all things to enjoy; That they do good, that they be rich in good works, ready to distribute, willing to communicate; Laying up in store for themselves a good foundation against the time to come, that they may lay hold on eternal life.* Paul instructs the rich people of this world not to be high-minded or conceited and not to trust in uncertain riches. Uncertain riches is referring to earthly wealth. Thus, he instructs them to put their trust in the living God. The last verse ends by saying that the rich should store up for themselves a good foundation that will last in the time to come so that they may lay hold on eternal life. In other words, amass heavenly treasures instead of earthly treasures, and embrace and prepare for eternal life.

Jesus tells a parable in the Bible of a rich man who had the wrong perspective. Luke 12:16-21 reads, *And he spake a parable unto them, saying, The ground of a certain rich man brought forth plentifully: ⁱ⁷ And he thought within himself, saying, What shall I do, because I have no room where to bestow my fruits? ⁱ⁸ And he said, This will I do: I will pull down my barns, and build greater; and there will I bestow all my fruits and my goods. ⁱ⁹ And I will say to my soul, Soul, thou hast much goods laid up for many years; take thine ease, eat, drink, and be merry. ²⁰ But God said unto him, Thou fool, this night thy soul shall be required of thee: then whose shall those things be, which thou hast provided? ²¹ So is he that layeth up treasure for himself, and is not rich toward God.* This rich man was blessed with many crops. However, his mind was focused on hoarding it for himself, and he decided to build bigger barns. Then, he planned to take it easy and relax for many years. Next, God called him a fool and told him that he would lose his life that very night. God asked him who would get all the "stuff" that he stored up here on earth. Jesus then says that this what will happen to those who store up treasure for themselves and are not rich toward God. Being rich toward God is being rich in eternal things. This should be our focus.

If we are honest with ourselves, many times we get stressed out by temporary things. We get stressed out about the car going out. We get stressed out about something bad that our kids have done. We get stressed out about where we should go to eat (If you're from New Orleans like me.) This does not mean that we abandon these things. They just should not be the center of our focus. The center of our focus should be eternal things. Anything that you do for God's kingdom is eternal. It can be evangelism, preaching, teaching, serving, giving, discipling, etc. Anything that God is calling you to do will be worth it in the long run!

The Apostle Paul wrote in Colossians 3:1-2, *If ye then be risen with Christ, seek those things which are above, where Christ sitteth on the right hand of God. ² Set your affection on things above, not on things on the earth.* Once again, Paul is teaching us where to set our affection or our minds. Our affections, our minds, and our thoughts should be on things above in Heaven where Christ is and not on things on the earth. This does not mean that we completely neglect our responsibilities on earth. It just means that our top priority is eternal things in Heaven with Jesus Christ. We should NOT say, "Oh well, that happened with my relationship with God through Jesus Christ, but I am fulfilled by my money and possessions." We should be able to say, "Oh well, that happened to my money and possessions, but I am fulfilled by my relationship with God through Jesus Christ." Our fulfillment should come from our reward of spending eternity in Heaven. If your security is in your money and possessions, then you will be in trouble on Judgment Day! Your security should be in your ETERNAL relationship with Jesus Christ, so D.E.T.A.C.H! Therefore, I will ask you again the same thing that I asked you in chapter 3. What are you ATTACHED to? Are you attached to the things of this world, which are temporary, or the things of God's Kingdom which are eternal?

Action Steps

After reading a book like this, you need to decide on some action steps to take. Let me summarize how you can develop a biblical mindset for personal finance. You need to commit to

D.E.T.A.C.H., examine yourself and figure out what you are attached to, set priorities and make God first place, determine to free yourself from debt, practice contentment, and live for God's kingdom. What if Christians, Churches, and Christian Organizations all over the world would truly D.E.T.A.C.H.? The result would be unparalleled in this 21st century! We would transform the world for Christ! Take some time right now to write down the actions steps that you will complete as a result of this book.

Complete the following statement for yourself. I choose to D.E.T.A.C.H. and detach from _____.

Invitation

Maybe you have been reading this book and you are not a follower of Jesus Christ. However, you sincerely want to become a follower of Jesus Christ and develop a personal relationship with God through Jesus Christ. If that's you, I would like to invite you to say this prayer with me to accept Jesus Christ as your personal Lord and Savior. "Dear God, I admit that I have sinned and messed up. I repent and turn away from my sins. Today, I place my trust in Jesus Christ as my Lord and Savior. I believe you sent your Son Jesus to die on the cross to pay the penalty for my sins and deliver me from your wrath to come. I believe you raised Jesus up from the dead on the 3rd day. Change my desires and help me to live the life that you want me to live. Please forgive me and give me your gift of everlasting life. Thank you for grace and thank you for saving me. In Jesus' name I pray, Amen." If you prayed that prayer and you truly meant it, I believe you have just become a Christian and a follower of Jesus Christ. CONGRATULATIONS! It is not so much the words, but your heart that matters when you pray a prayer to accept Jesus Christ as your Lord and Savior. If you have taken this step, I want to hear from you. I would love to get you some free resources to help you as you begin your new life in Christ. Contact me through our ministry's website at www.kingdomfinancial.org. God bless you!

> *"Financial freedom is having the ability to give generously, save sufficiently, and serve skillfully in the Kingdom of God."*
> –Jonathan Sayles

ABOUT THE AUTHOR

Jonathan Sayles is President of Kingdom Financial Education, which is a 501(c)(3) Christian nonprofit ministry that teaches individuals and families how to handle money God's way. Jonathan has multiple years of financial services experience including helping and teaching individuals about budgeting, insurance, saving, debt, retirement planning, stewardship, and more. Mr. Sayles received a Bachelor of Science in Finance and a Master of Business Administration degree from the University of

New Orleans. Also, he is the author of *Kingdom Financial* College, which is an 8-week course that teaches you how to manage your money based on the Bible. He is a follower of Jesus Christ and upholds biblical values. Jonathan is married to Jessica Sayles, and they have one daughter, Joanna. They live in the New Orleans, LA area.

APPENDIX

Personal Balance Sheet	
ASSETS (What You Own)	
Cash/Checking	$
Savings	$
Jewelry	$
Furniture	$
Retirement Accounts	$
Investments	$
Business Valuation (Current Value)	$
Automobiles/Boats	$
Primary Home	$
Other Real Estate	$
Other_____	$
Other_____	$
TOTAL ASSETS	$
LIABILITIES (What You Owe)	
Primary Home Mortgage	$
Home Equity Line of Credit	$
Other Real Estate Loans	$
Automobile/Boat Loans	$
Student Loans	$
Credit Card Debt	$
Personal loans	$
Business Loans	$
Other Loans_____	$
Other Debt_____	$
TOTAL LIABILITIES	$
NET WORTH (total assets minus liabilities)	$

Debt Snowball

Item	Balance	Minimum Payment	Total Payment	Interest Rate

Instructions: List your debts smallest to largest. Pay minimum payments on all debts except the smallest one. Add all extra money to the smallest debt. When you pay it off, you add that amount to the next smallest debt and so on until you have paid all debts.

Household Spending Plan

		Monthly	Annual
Income	Total Household Income	$	$
Taxes	Federal	$	$
	State	$	$
	Local	$	$
	TOTAL	$	$
Giving	Church (Tithe)	$	$
	Charitable	$	$
	Holidays, birthdays, anniversary	$	$
	TOTAL	$	$
Saving	Personal/Emergency	$	$
	Retirement/Investments	$	$
	TOTAL	$	$
Housing	Mortgage/Rent	$	$
	Homeowners/Renters Insurance	$	$
	Property Taxes	$	$
	Flood Insurance	$	$
	Repairs/Maintenance	$	$
	HOA Dues/Fees	$	$
	TOTAL	$	$
Utilities	Electricity	$	$
	Gas	$	$
	Water	$	$
	Phone/Cell Phone	$	$
	Cable/Internet	$	$
	TOTAL	$	$
Auto	Car Note	$	$
	Gasoline	$	$
	Insurance	$	$
	Parking/Tolls/Transit	$	$
	License/Registration	$	$
	Maintenance/Repairs	$	$
	Other	$	$
	TOTAL	$	$

Category	Item		
General	Food/Groceries	$	$
	Clothing	$	$
	Cleaning products/supplies	$	$
	Other	$	$
	Barber/Beauty	$	$
	TOTAL	$	$
Health/Medical	Health Insurance	$	$
	Dental Insurance	$	$
	Life Insurance	$	$
	Disability Insurance	$	$
	Long Term Care Insurance	$	$
	Prescription/OTC drugs	$	$
	Other Medical Expenses	$	$
	TOTAL	$	$
Children	Child Care	$	$
	Education	$	$
	Other	$	$
	TOTAL	$	$
Entertainment	Dining Out	$	$
	Travel	$	$
	Hobbies (golf, fishing, hunting)	$	$
	Club dues (country club/social)	$	$
	Tickets/sporting events	$	$
	Gym Membership	$	$
	Other	$	$
	TOTAL	$	$
Debt	Credit Cards	$	$
	Student Loans	$	$
	Home Equity Line of Credit	$	$
	Personal Loans	$	$
	Other (Specify)	$	$
	TOTAL	$	$
	TOTAL LIVING EXPENSES	$	$
-	INCOME	$	$
	SURPLUS OR DEFICIT	$	$

Irregular Income Spending Plan (Example)

Item	Amount	Cumulative Total
Tithe	$ 300.00	$ 300.00
Other Giving	$ 30.00	$ 330.00
Savings	$ 150.00	$ 480.00
Food	$ 100.00	$ 580.00
Mortgage/Rent	$ 600.00	$ 1,180.00
Electricity	$ 50.00	$ 1,230.00
Transportation	$ 450.00	$ 1,680.00

Irregular Income Spending Plan

Item	Amount	Cumulative Total

ENDNOTES

1. Jim Forsyth, "More Than Two-thirds in U.S. Live Paycheck to Paycheck: Survey," *Reuters*, September 19, 2012, http://www.reuters.com/article/2012/09/19/us-usa-survey-paycheck-idUS-BRE88I1BE20120919.
2. Nanci Hellmich, "Retirement: A Third Have Less Than $1,000 Put Away," *USA Today*, April 1, 2014, http://www.usatoday.com/story/money/personal-finance/2014/03/18/ retirement-confidence-survey-savings/6432241/.
3. Mike Holmes, "What Would Happen if the Church Tithed? How Giving 10 Percent Could Change the World," *Relevant Magazine*, July 10, 2013, http://www.relevantmagazine.com/god/church/what-would-happen-if-church-tithed.

Also from Jonathan Sayles:
Kingdom Financial College

Kingdom Financial College is a life transforming, biblically-based course that teaches individuals and families how to handle their finances God's ways. It combines biblical financial principles with practical applications. This course 1) Teaches a biblical view of stewardship, 2) Equips you to eliminate debt, 3) Trains you to manage a budget and plan your spending, 4) Helps you to develop a savings plan, and 5) Provides a long-term strategy that gives hope for those that are struggling with their finances. The workbook is the text that goes along with the *Kingdom Financial College* DVD.

To learn more visit kingdomfinancial.org

CPSIA information can be obtained at www.ICGtesting.com
Printed in the USA
LVOW07s0907260815
451531LV00018B/109/P